Independent Living Services
for Youths in Out-of-Home Care

Madelyn DeWoody
Kathy Ceja
Megan Sylvester

CHILD WELFARE LEAGUE OF AMERICA • WASHINGTON, DC

© 1993 by the Child Welfare League of America, Inc.

CHILD WELFARE LEAGUE OF AMERICA, INC.
440 First Street, NW, Suite 310, Washington, DC 20001-2085

CURRENT PRINTING (last digit)
10 9 8 7 6 5 4 3 2 1

Cover design by Jennifer Riggs
Text design by Eve Malakoff-Klein

Printed in the United States of America

ISBN # 0–87868–582–0

Contents

Acknowledgments

The authors wish to acknowledge the following individuals for their significant contributions to this report: Lisa Merkel for her substantive contributions and editorial assistance throughout the development of this report; Nickola Dixon for her word processing expertise, which made this document possible; and Eve Malakoff-Klein for her editing of this report.

Introduction

Youths living in out-of-home care are very much like their peers living with their parents or other kin. Like their peers, they need assistance as they begin to establish themselves as adults. Like their peers, they have strengths that must be supported if they are to successfully make the transition to adulthood. And like their peers, at age 18, they do not magically become self-supporting and self-sufficient.

At the same time, however, youths in out-of-home care have special vulnerabilities and may need help and support that extend beyond that typically provided to youths cared for by parents or kin. Youths leaving out-of-home care may have histories of abuse, neglect, or exploitation that can compromise their ability to live independently. Upon discharge from out-of-home care, they find themselves on their own, with scarce financial resources; limited education, training, and employment options; and no place to live. These young persons are often expected to accomplish at age 18 what many other youths rarely do at such an age: establish themselves independently as adults. While youths who are not in care often continue to live with their families well past the age of 18, receiving ongoing financial, emotional, and social support, or freely returning home if initial efforts at independence are unsuccessful, their counterparts in out-of-home care often lack such options. These youths lack the safety net of family and social supports and are unaware of or lack access to the community resources that might help them meet the challenges they face.

Adjustment to adulthood and independence may be particularly difficult for youths in out-of-home care because the protective environment of out-of-home care may not have prepared them for self-sufficiency and independence. A youth's status as a "client" of the child welfare system may mean that other people, including many the young person has never met, have made all the important decisions in the youth's life.*

The critical challenge facing the child welfare system is to prepare the youths in its care for independence and self-sufficiency. These young people need the support of understanding, responsive, and committed adults; services designed to prepare them for self-sufficiency; and access to a range of community resources that can readily meet the needs that all young adults have.

This monograph reviews the needs of youths in out-of-home care who are making the transition to independent living; assesses the federal Independent Living Program, the resources that the program has brought to the child welfare field, the projects it has supported, and the gaps that continue to exist; reports on the results of a survey of youth-serving agencies conducted by the Child Welfare League of America in late 1992; and sets forth recommendations for the further development and support of independent living services. It is our hope that it will provoke thought and action on the part of program developers, policymakers, youth advocates, and all who are committed to helping adolescents in out-of-home care make the transition into successful and productive adulthood.

David S. Liederman
Executive Director
Child Welfare League of America

---

* Cook, R. "Trends and Needs in Programming for Independent Living," in *Independent Living Services for At-Risk Adolescents* (*Child Welfare* Special Issue), edited by E.V. Mech (Washington, DC: Child Welfare League of America, 1988), 498–499.

SECTION I

Youths in Out-of-Home Care:
A Status Report

Adolescents constitute a major segment of the population served by the child welfare system. In 1989, over one-third of all children in out-of-home care were teens.[1] Although demographic information about youths in out-of-home care is limited, a few generalizations can be made:

1.   Youths in out-of-home care are racially and culturally diverse.

Adolescents of color, like children of color of all ages, are proportionately overrepresented in the child welfare system.[2] Although the majority of youths in out-of-home care are Caucasian,[3] a significant portion of the population is African American, Latino, or Native American. In 1983, for example, African American children and youths under the age of 19 comprised only 14 percent of the general population. However, they represented 33 percent of all children and youths in out-of-home care.[4]

Westat, Inc., in its pioneering survey of the characteristics of youths leaving family foster care and other forms of out-of-home care between January 1987 and July 1988, found that members of racial and ethnic minority groups comprised almost 40 percent of the youths leaving care.[5] Thirty percent were African American, 4 percent were Latino/Hispanic, and 1 percent were Native American.[6]

2.   *More children leave care as adolescents than at any other age.*

Of the children who left out-of-home care in fiscal year 1988, 42.9 percent were between the ages of 13 and 18 years, 24 percent were children ages six to 12, 24 percent were children ages one to five, and 5 percent were infants.[7] Unlike other age groups, youth ages 13 to 18 tend to leave out-of-home care in greater numbers than they enter care.[8] Although approximately one-half leave care to live with relatives, those who do not face the real prospect of living independently.[9] Their need for supportive environments after discharge from care must be recognized and addressed

3.   *As youths remain in out-of-home care for longer periods of time, increasing numbers of them plan to live independently upon discharge rather than return to their families as initially planned.*

In the Westat study, researchers found that the initial permanency planning goal for the majority of youths was reunification with parents and relatives (61 percent) with only 17 percent of the youths having independent living as the initial goal. Prior to discharge, however, 38 percent of the youths had independent living as a goal and only 34 percent had reunification as the permanent plan.[10]

4.   *Many youths leaving out-of-home care at age 18 do not have the support of their families.*

Existing data is inconsistent regarding the number of adolescents in out-of-home care who return home after discharge. The Westat study found that 54 percent of youths leaving out-of-home care lived with extended families members at the time of their discharge.[11] Other researchers, however, have found that fewer than 20 percent of the adolescents in out-of-home care actually return home after discharge.[12] Regardless of the actual number of adolescents who return home, studies do agree that many adolescents leaving out-of-home care at age 18 lack ongoing support from their families and need other support systems to help them move toward self-sufficiency.

5.   *Youths in out-of-home care often have experiences in care that affect their successful transition to adulthood.*

Most youths in out-of-home care entered care as adolescents. The

Westat study found that over 70 percent of youths in out-of-home care entered care as teenagers, with approximately 30 percent entering at age 16 or older.[13] The younger the youth is at time of entry into care, however, the longer the stay in out-of-home care tends to be. The Westat study found that the median length of time in care for youths under the age of 13 entering out-of-home care was nine years, in contrast to two and one-half years for youths who entered between the ages of 13 and 15, and one year for youths who entered at age 16 or older.[14]

In addition to remaining in care for significant periods of time, many youths also experience multiple placements while in care. In the Westat study, 58 percent of the youths had experienced three or more living arrangements during the time they spent in out-of-home care; 14 percent had five or more living arrangements.[15] Forty-five percent of the youths had run away from an out-of-home placement at least once.[16] Extended stays in out-of-home care and multiple placements may have profound developmental consequences for young people and affect their ability to build a solid foundation for adulthood.

Backgrounds of Youths in Out-of-Home Care

Studies of youths in care are scarce and yield results that are not definitive, existing studies of the reasons that children and youths enter out-of-home care document the troubled backgrounds these children have experienced—backgrounds characterized by instability, abuse, neglect, and rejection. A 1984 study by the California Association of Services for Children of the family histories of 9,977 California children and youths in out-of-home care found that the children and youths entered care because of neglect (30 percent), physical abuse (25 percent), sexual abuse (9.5 percent), psychological abuse (17.1 percent), parental substance abuse (19.3 percent), and the inability of the parent to care for him/herself (10.4 percent).*

In the Westat study, the specific factors most frequently identified in

---

*   The actual rate may be greater, as these results do not reflect the full impact of the increase in parental alcohol and drug use, which has contributed significantly to the growing number of children and youths in care over the last several years.

the youths' parental histories were inadequate parenting skills (59 percent), physical neglect (34 percent), physical abuse (32 percent), parental alcohol abuse (31 percent), emotional neglect (29 percent), emotional abuse (26 percent), sexual abuse (17 percent), abandonment (17 percent), drug abuse by parents (14 percent), parental mental illness (13 percent), spouse abuse (10 percent), parental incarceration (7 percent), and parental mental retardation (5 percent).[17] It should be noted that many of the youths faced a multiplicity of problems at home. In the Westat study, for example, 35 percent of the families had a history of four or more of the above factors.[18]

One particularly vulnerable group within the population of youths served by child welfare agencies is the estimated one million adolescents who run away from home or become homeless each year. These youngsters often have extremely troubled backgrounds. A 1991 survey by the National Association of Social Workers (NASW) of 360 agencies serving runaway and homeless youths found that risk factors for runaway behavior by young people were neglect, abuse, parental substance abuse, emotional conflict, child substance abuse, and poor school performance combined with low self-esteem.[19] More than 60 percent of the youngsters in shelters and transitional living facilities had been physically or sexually abused; 25 percent had experienced violence from family members other than parents.[20] The survey also found significant rates of substance abuse among the parents of runaway and homeless youths: alcohol problems were present among the parents of 29 percent of the youths and drug abuse was a problem for the parents of 24 percent of the youths.[21]

Needs of Youths in Out-of-Home Care

The Westat evaluation of independent living programs found that youths discharged from out-of-home care had a number of significant needs that could affect their ability to lead productive lives as adults after discharge from care. Problems included a lack of educational achievement, few job skills or experience, physical and mental health issues, and unmet housing needs.[23]

- Only 48 percent of 18- and 19-year-olds studied had completed high school, compared to 64 percent nationwide.

- Only 30 percent of youths leaving care had held at least one part-time job by the time of discharge. In contrast, over 55 percent of youths nationwide aged 16 to 19 have held jobs.

- Forty-seven percent of the adolescents in care had a disabling condition and 37 percent were clinically diagnosed as emotionally disturbed, percentages much higher than the 12 percent to 15 percent estimate for the general population of children and youths.

- Seventeen percent of the youths reported drug problems and 12 percent reported alcohol abuse problems. Actual levels are likely to be considerably higher.

- Seventeen percent of the girls had been pregnant at least once by the time of discharge and over 60 percent had at least one child within four years of discharge. In contrast, only 25 percent of women age 18 to 24 in the general population have a child.

- Sixteen percent of the youths had been sexually abused.

- Nine percent of the youths reported health problems that required ongoing medical care after discharge.

The NASW survey of runaway and homeless youths documented similar problems among young people served by emergency shelters. More than one-half (53 percent) had educational problems, 26 percent had a mental health problem and 20 percent had attempted suicide, 23 percent had abused drugs and 19 percent had abused alcohol, 23 percent had been sexually abused by a parent, and 37 percent had no means of support.[24]

Research by Festinger in 1983 also identified the service needs of youths in out-of-home care. She found that youths discharged from out-of-home care in New York City required ongoing planning and services after discharge because of traumatic prior life experiences:

- Many youths had multiple placements throughout their stays in out-of-home care.

- Many youths had fallen behind educationally, as changes in placement often necessitated transfers to new schools.

- Thirty-four percent of the young adults had exited out-of-home care with a fairly serious health, social, emotional, or educational problem, or some combination of these problems.

- Thirty percent of the youths exiting care were uncertain about who could be counted upon to help them, although many identified someone who could provide advice.

- Approximately 32 percent of the males and nearly 5 percent of the females surveyed had been arrested on a misdemeanor or felony charge at some point following discharge from out-of-home care.[25]

Independent Living Services

Young people in out-of-home care need preparation in basic living skills—how to find a place to live, budget and manage money, pay bills, obtain a driver's license, prepare meals, develop friendships and supportive relationships, and take care of their personal needs. Of particular importance in preparing youths for independent living are services that focus on educational attainment, employment, and career preparation.[26]

The Child Welfare League of America's *Standards for Independent-Living Services* recognize that youths in out-of-home care must acquire a number of basic living skills. The *Standards* set forth the independent living services that must be provided to enable each youth to acquire those skills. These services, targeted at enhancing the ability of youths to live independently and self-sufficiently, include social work services such as individual, group, and family counseling services;[27] educational services;[28] employment services;[29] health services;[30] housing services;[31] legal services;[32] social, cultural, and recreational services;[33] and aftercare services that support youths after they leave out-of-home care.[34]

The *Standards* also provide a framework for independent living services that can be used to assess the extent to which the services youths need are currently being provided. In 1992, using the *Standards* as a guide, CWLA surveyed its member agencies that provide independent living services to youths to learn—from the perspective of youth-serving agencies themselves—about the services provided and the services needed by youths preparing for independent living. One hundred three agencies responded, providing information about the range of services that youths need and the extent to which agencies currently are able to provide service to support young people as they move into life on their own.

The material below, which follows the framework of independent living services established in the CWLA *Standards*, explores the types of services needed by youths as they prepare for independence, the need for each type of service as reflected by research, and the extent to which each type of service is currently available, as indicated by the survey responses.

Educational Services.

CWLA's *Standards for Independent Living Services* identify the need for an array of educational services for youths in out-of-home care :[35]

- Educational services should begin with informal and formal assessments of skills, learning styles, aptitudes, and abilities.

- Educational assessments should assist adolescents in determining the appropriate educational resource needed and in gaining access to that resource.

- For youth with disabilities in out-of-home care, efforts should be made to ensure that the resources and entitlements provided by P.L. 94-142 (The Individuals with Disabilities Education Act) are available.

Supporting the need for these services are a number of studies that link educational attainment directly to success in independent living. For example, in a study by the Carnegie Council on Adolescent Development of 709 youth-serving organizations, agencies consistently identified better or alternative schooling as one of the services most needed by youths.[36] Likewise, the Westat study found that completion of high school by youths in out-of-home care led to better outcomes for the youths in terms of holding a job for one year or longer after discharge from out-of-home care, not being a cost to the community, and overall self-sufficiency.[37]

Despite the importance of education to their future, however, youths in out-of-home care are at risk of falling behind educationally. A 1986 study by Cook and Ansell found that only 28 percent of 257 adolescents surveyed had completed high school or obtained a GED upon discharge from out-of-home care.[38] Although a later study of 18- and 19-year-olds showed that a higher rate (48 percent) had completed high school or obtained a GED upon discharge,[39] both figures compare unfavorably to the 64 percent of 18- and 19-year-olds in the general population who have completed high school.[40] A 1987 study by the Ohio Department of Human Services found that 48 percent of Ohio school children in out-of-home care were below grade level in reading and more than half performed below grade level in math.[41]

In addition to high school and GED completion, the Westat evaluation of independent living services focused on other indicators of educational achievement that may affect the ability of youths in out-of-home care to function independently as adults.[42] Although case records frequently did not include the desired information, Westat researchers found that:

- Of the 43 percent of youths for whom such information was available, 19 percent had repeated a grade.

- Of the 70 percent of youths for whom such information was available, 30 percent required special educational placement services.

- Of the 61 percent of youths for whom such information was available, 11 percent had had a "drop out" period of at least three months.[43]

Additionally, case records revealed that only 44 percent of the youths received specific assistance in educational planning.[44]

Educational achievement after discharge from out-of-home care is a significant issue not just for the child welfare system but for the youths themselves. Many young people who leave out-of-home care complete high school after formally leaving school. The Westat study, for example, found that the proportion of 18-year-olds who had completed high school was 43 percent at the time of discharge from out-of-home care but nearly 54 percent two to four years later.[45] Educational achievement of this group, however, remains considerably lower than the national norm of nearly 80 percent of persons aged 18 to 24 who have completed high school.[46]

In her 1983 study, Festinger found that youths who had been in out-of-home care were significantly less likely to complete college than the general population of New York City youths—young men who had been in care completed college at a rate of only 2.3 percent as compared to 22.1 percent for the general population.[47]

The CWLA survey revealed that many agencies provide services to help meet youths' educational needs. Twenty percent of the agencies responding assess skills and learning styles and develop educational plans for youths in their care, 14 percent of the agencies refer youths to college classes and vocational training within the community, and 10 percent advocate in behalf of the youths, including providing help in obtaining educational entitlements. Other educational services that agencies provide included tutoring (18 percent); career counseling (14 percent); and financial assistance to help youths obtain needed educational services (9 percent).

Job Experience and Employment Services

Employment services are an important component of preparation for independent living. CWLA's *Standards* state that these services should include:

- an assessment of the youth's ability to find employment independently;

- an assessment of the youth's strengths, needs, abilities, and limitations related to work and the sharing of this experience with the youth;

- use of all available community employment and training resources and assistance in accessing those resources;

- assistance for hard-to-employ youths in developing the work habits, self-awareness, and social skills needed to obtain and hold a job; and

- development of job leads in the private sector and working with potential employers of young people.[48]

The Westat study illustrates the critical need for these services. The study found that 39 percent of the youths surveyed had held at least one job while in out-of-home care, a figure considerably lower than the employment rate for the general youth population.[49] Case records revealed that only 38 percent of youths received specific assistance in developing job-seeking skills and only 30 percent received assistance in developing job maintenance skills.[50]

Upon discharge, youths who have been in out-of-home care find it more difficult to obtain employment than youths in general. The Westat follow-up study of youths who had left out-of-home care found that 49 percent of respondents were employed, whereas the national employment level for young people ages 16 to 24 years during the same time period was over 65 percent.[51] Another indicator of employment among youths discharged from out-of-home care is independence from reliance on welfare. The same follow-up study by Westat found that the proportion of youths discharged from out-of-home care who were receiving welfare was eight times the level of that in the general population of 16- to 24-year-olds.[52]

Fewer than one-quarter of the CWLA member agencies responding to the survey reported providing employment-related services for youths in their care. Seventeen percent indicated that they provided assessments relating to employment and career planning, 16 percent provided training in job search skills, 24 percent provided vocational skills training, and 28 percent had a job coach or counselor available.

Skills in Living on One's Own

CWLA's *Standards for Independent Living Services* emphasize that the following basic living skills must be supported and enhanced through independent living programs:

- basic survival skills, including locating needed resources (police, dentist, a lawyer, clergy, banker, insurance), connecting with community resources (churches, recreational activities, caring adults), and gaining access to peer support groups;[53]

- money management skills;[54]

- skills in personal decision making;[55]

- skills in obtaining, and maintaining a residence, including locating a residence, negotiating a lease, and home management skills, (i.e., food preparation, laundry, cleaning, living cooperatively, basic maintenance, simple repairs);[56]

• personal care skills;[57] and

• skills in locating and using community resources to meet individual needs.[58]

The *Standards* also state that the development of these skills must be enhanced by individual, group, and family counseling services that prepare youths for the future.[59]

Unfortunately, less than half of the youths discharged from out-of-home care receive assistance in developing specific skills that will enable them to live on their own.[60] In his study of 55 youths who left out-of-home care in the San Francisco Bay area, Barth found that most did not participate in independent living preparation prior to leaving care. Sixty-nine percent reported that they had received no assistance in learning how to budget money and 22 percent stated that they did not know how to use public transportation when they were discharged from care.[61] Similarly, the Westat study found that only 7 percent of the youths surveyed had lived in an independent arrangement, such as a supervised or semi-supervised apartment, before their discharge from care.[62] The study also reviewed case records to determine whether youths received training in a number of skill areas related to independent living. Table one summarizes the findings for several skill areas.

The CWLA survey indicated that agencies generally provide basic living skills training through workshops, seminars, and classes. The topics covered in such sessions included: hygiene and general health (28 percent), accessing medical care and insurance (10 percent), legal assistance in reading housing agreements and legal documents such as credit card applications (30 percent), legal rights and responsibilities (30 percent), food preparation and nutrition (16 percent), and locating and renting apartments and tenant/landlord rights (22 percent).

Contact with Family

CWLA's *Standards for Independent Living Services* promote the role of the family of origin in actively supporting the youth whenever possible in developing independent living skills while in care and as he or she moves toward independence.[64] The *Standards* recommend:

TABLE ONE

Percentage of Youths Receiving Independent Living Services in Specific Skill Areas*

Skill Area	Services Received/ Reported in Record	Services Not Received/Not Reported in Record
Money Management/ Consumer Awareness	32%	68%
Decision Making/ Problem Solving Skills	31%	69%
Food Management	29%	71%
Knowledge of Community Resources	29%	71%
Housing	24%	76%
Emergency and Safety Skills	18%	82%

The more active families can be in supporting their children in developing these [independent living] skills while they are in out-of-home care, the better. In some situations, the agency may need to help young persons accept the probability that their family may never be able to provide the desired emotional, financial, or psychological support. When appropriate, the agency should attempt to keep the family informed of changes in the child's life and progress toward the goal of independent living.[65]

The Westat study supports the importance of family involvement in the lives of youths. In contrast to plans for reunification with family or relatives, independent living became the permanent plan for a number of youths *after* they entered out-of-home care. Yet even when reunification as the goal for the youth was changed to independent living, parental involvement in the young person's life continued at some level. Parental rights were terminated in less than 10 percent of the cases.[66] In addition, 69

---

*   Adapted from Westat, Inc., *A National Evaluation of Title IV-E Foster Care Independent Living Programs for Youth, Phase I, Final Report* (Rockville, MD: Westat, 1988), 1: 4–23.

percent of the youths reported visiting at least once with their mothers and 47 percent reported visiting at least once with their fathers during the last year in out-of-home care.[67]

These findings suggest that contact with family is important to youths, irrespective of the permanent plan at the time of discharge. Likewise, child welfare professionals have observed that even when agencies change the permanent plan from reunification to independent living in the belief that return to the family is not a viable option, young people often return to parents, extended family, and friends of family after discharge from out-of-home care. As the Carnegie Council on Adolescent Development Study found, youths have a critical need for parental and familial support and the fostering of a positive relationship with their families.[68]

The CWLA survey did not specifically ask agencies about the extent of their contact with the families of youths in their care. However, 14 percent of the responding agencies stated that they provided family counseling. It is possible that agencies involve family members in other ways with the youths they serve, although anecdotal accounts suggest that families often are not a focus in independent living programs.

Health Care

CWLA's *Standards for Independent Living Services* focus on the need for an array of health care services for youths preparing for independent living, including assuring the continuity of health care after discharge from out-of-home care. Upon leaving care, young people need to know how to identify and gain access to health care services and must be given their complete medical records and history.[69]

As is true for all youths, services must be designed and provided to address the interrelated issues of sexual activity, chemical dependency, and HIV infection. CWLA's *Standards* specifically recognize the need to incorporate services concerning these issues as an integral part of any independent living program. The *Standards* recommend that services assist adolescents to:

- develop a sense of responsibility for their own sexual behavior[70] including responsible family planning, adolescent pregnancy prevention,[71] and an understanding of HIV infection and AIDS,[72] and

- understand chemical dependency so as to live a dependency-free, productive life.[73]

The need for health care services is supported by the Westat study, which revealed that only 36 percent of youths were provided with specific assistance related to health care in preparation for independent living.[74] Specific assistance included efforts to educate the youths about the need for primary care, preventive care, specialized medical services, and how to gain access to health care services after discharge from care.

One specific area that often is not addressed in adolescent health programs in general, nor in independent living programs, is the "triple threat" to youths from sexual activity, chemical dependency and infection from the human immunodeficiency virus (HIV)—the virus that causes AIDS. Research regarding the status of youths with regard to chemical dependency, sexual activity, and HIV infection dramatically illustrates the need for health education, prevention, and treatment services.

CHEMICAL DEPENDENCY

Statistical information on chemical dependency among youths in out-of-home care is extremely limited. The Barth study and the Westat evaluation, however, give some measure of the problem for youths in out-of-home care. Barth found that 19 percent of youths responding to his survey drank alcohol while in out-of-home care—a rate comparable to a random sample of high school students—but 56 percent reported using street drugs, a much higher rate than the general population of high school students,[75] and 56 percent continued to use drugs after leaving care.[76] The Westat study indicated that 17 percent of youths discharged from out-of-home care reported drug problems and 12 percent reported alcohol problems at the time of discharge. Child welfare experts generally agree that these statistics, like most data reflecting alcohol and drug use among adolescents, understate the problem.[77]

Perhaps the best currently available information on chemical dependency relates to adolescents as a group. The National Institute on Drug Abuse (NIDA), in one of the most comprehensive studies currently available, reports that 54 percent of high school seniors admitted that they had tried an illicit drug by the time of graduation and 35 percent reported drinking heavily in the past two weeks.[78] While reported cocaine use decreased to 12 percent from the previous year's level of 15 percent, crack cocaine use remained at over 3 percent.[79] Another NIDA study of juniors and seniors revealed that 8 million youths (nearly 40 percent) consume alcohol weekly; 5.4 million "binge" (drink five or more drinks in a row); and 454,000 report averaging 15 drinks each week.[80] The Center for Population Options found that substance abuse begins at a young age for many youths. Of the high school seniors who reported using cocaine, for example, 33 percent said they had begun using alcohol at age 11 or younger.[81]

HIV/AIDS

It is difficult to precisely describe the impact of AIDS and HIV infection on youths in out-of-home care, but the threat to these youngsters is clearly illustrated by recent data on the growing numbers of young people who have been diagnosed as HIV infected or as having AIDS.* From June 1989 to January 1991, the number of AIDS cases reported among 13- to 19-year-olds doubled (from 389 to 646). The number of reported cases among 20- to 29-year-olds rose from 20,545 to 31,675 cases—fully 20 percent of all reported cases since the epidemic began.[82]

Of all AIDS cases reported by April 30, 1991, one in five was a young adult in his or her twenties. Because of the average eight- to ten-year latency period for the disease, most of these adults were likely infected as teenagers. The total number of AIDS cases among young persons ages 13 to 24 increased by 75 percent between 1989 and 1990.[83]

HIV infection is increasing among youths. It is estimated that by the end of 1991, there were between 10,000 and 20,000 symptomatic HIV-infected infants, children, and youths.[84] A recent study of youths in Washington, DC showed that the HIV infection rate had soared from 4.07 per 1,000 youths ages 13 to 19 to 13.05 per 1,000 over the four-year period of 1987 to 1991.[85]

SEXUAL ACTIVITY

Studies suggest that young people in out-of-home care engage in sexual activity at high rates and, consequently, may be particularly

---

* Human immunodeficiency virus (HIV) is the virus that causes acquired immune deficiency syndrome (AIDS). HIV may be clinically silent for years before AIDS develops and is diagnosed.

susceptible to unintended pregnancy and sexually transmitted diseases. In the Barth study, 91 percent of young people responding stated that they were sexually active one year after discharge from out-of-home care, 40 percent reported having a pregnancy since leaving out-of-home care, and 17 percent stated that they had acquired a sexually transmitted disease post foster care.[86] In the Westat study, 42 percent of the youths responding had either given birth to or fathered a child.[87] While 60 percent of the females in out-of-home care had given birth within two to four years of discharge from care, only 24 percent of the males had fathered a child, suggesting that gender is a key factor in developing programs that assist youths in avoiding early parenthood.[88] Only 25 percent of the general population aged 18 to 24 had given birth.[89] Another study of young women aged 13 to 18 found that those in out-of-home care were 50 percent more likely to report having sex and were significantly less informed about birth control than those not in care.[90]

Rates of sexual activity among all youths is rising. Studies reflect that 78 percent of adolescent girls and 86 percent of adolescent boys have engaged in sexual intercourse by age 20; the percentage of boys and girls ages 15 to 19 who are sexually active is also rising.[91] Likewise, teen pregnancy is on the rise[92] and substantial numbers of teens fail to use contraceptives at the time of first intercourse.[93] These trends suggest that youths in out-of-home care, like other youths, are increasingly at risk for unintended pregnancies and other consequences of sexual activity, including HIV infection and other sexually transmitted diseases (STDs).

INTERRELATIONSHIPS AMONG SEXUAL ACTIVITY, CHEMICAL DEPENDENCY, AND HIV/AIDS

The interrelationship of sexual activity, substance abuse, and HIV/AIDS is particularly important for youths in out-of-home care. Because many of these youths have suffered physical or sexual abuse, they are often at higher risk of engaging in sexual activity or alcohol or other drug use than their peers in the general population,[94] with the attendant dangers of acquiring HIV or other sexually transmitted diseases. Factors that influence inappropriate decision-making regarding alcohol and drug use and sexual behavior include abusive home situations, peer pressure, low self-esteem, and a perception of having limited options.[95] The presence of these factors, combined with the developmental needs of adolescents, including the dynamics of an evolving sense of self, experimentation, and dependence on peers, underline the need for targeted services for youths in care.

Forty-two percent of those responding to the CWLA survey provided health education, 18 percent provided training on HIV and other sexually transmitted diseases, and one program offered HIV testing. Seventeen percent offered training on sexuality issues, including pregnancy prevention, and 7 percent offered drug education classes. Additionally, 34 percent of the agencies indicated that they routinely refer youths to appropriate medical care in the community, and two programs stated that they provide transportation to medical appointments. Ninety percent of the respondents required yearly physical examinations of the children and youths in their charge.

Aftercare

CWLA's *Standards for Independent Living Services* advise agencies to take a number of steps in developing aftercare programs for youths moving from out-of-home care to independent living. The *Standards* focus on the need to develop aftercare services that include financial assistance, employment counseling and support, crisis counseling, emergency shelter, housing assistance, information and referral, community service opportunities, peer support programs, and advocacy.[96] The *Standards* also highlight the involvement of community institutions in assisting youths in moving toward self-sufficiency and recommend that agencies:

> use such teaching technologies as modeling, group presentation, individual tutoring, experiential learning, problem-solving, and counseling to show adolescents how best to find and take advantage of the resources available through community agencies.[97]

The Westat study broadly defined aftercare as services received by youths after they were discharged from out-of-home care. Using this definition, it found that 30 percent of the surveyed youths received aftercare services. The scope of these services, however, varied. For most, aftercare meant follow-up appointments with caseworkers; for a smaller number, aftercare included linkage with community volunteers and educational scholarships.[98] Consistent with the Westat findings, others have observed that aftercare services for youths leaving out-of-home care have generally been "hit or miss," depending on whether caseworkers have sufficient time to provide these services, whether a youth calls the caseworker, and whether, given the staff turnover prevalent in some agencies, the worker is still there.[99]

The CWLA survey revealed that 16 percent of the respondents provide some type of aftercare services to youths for some period of time after discharge. Five percent stated that they provide aftercare for one year; 10 percent for six months; and 6 percent for three months. Thirteen percent reported that they have staff who are available to discharged youths who choose to return to the program for periodic guidance and consultation. Seven percent of the programs stated that they provide no aftercare services.

Housing

CWLA's *Standards for Independent Living Services* emphasize the importance of housing services in assisting youths in making a successful transition to independence. Efforts to assist youths in locating suitable living arrangements should include:

- education about the key factors in choosing housing;
- exploration of the range of housing options based on personal needs and budget;
- education about health and safety standards, tenants' rights, and renters' responsibilities to the landlord and the community; and
- advocacy to ensure that adequate, affordable housing is available to adolescents seeking independent living.[100]

The *Standards* state that a prerequisite for discharge is the identification of a home for the adolescent, and that "under no circumstances should an adolescent be discharged into homelessness."[101]

In the Westat study, only 24 percent of the youths discharged from out-of-home care received housing services.[102] In its preliminary study conducted in 1986, Westat had found that the extent to which housing services were available depended on the state in which the youth resided.[103]

That study revealed that the percentage of youths receiving housing information varied from a low of 8 percent in one state to a high of 66 percent in another state.[104]

According to the more recent Westat study, at time of discharge, most youths (54 percent) moved in with extended family. Others remained with the foster family (10 percent), lived alone or with a child (17 percent), lived with a significant other (7 percent), or lived with unrelated individuals (12 percent). Through a follow-up study two and one-half to four years after discharge, researchers learned that 38 percent of the youths were living with extended family, as compared to 52.3 percent of all 18- to 24-year-olds in the general population.[105] Approximately 25 percent had spent at least one night without a place to live.[106] For the majority of the youths who had experienced a homeless episode, homelessness was related to a lack of personal resources in a time of crisis.[107]

In response to the CWLA survey, 24 percent of the agencies stated that they provided education concerning key factors in choosing housing, such as the range of housing options available based on personal needs and budget, and tenants' rights and responsibilities. Forty percent of the surveyed programs reported that they provided assistance in locating and securing housing.

Other Services

CWLA's *Standards for Independent Living Services* recognize the need for a range of additional services for youths. One area of need is access to legal services "to protect and promote the rights of young people in their efforts to adjust to community living."[108] At the same time, youths also need social, cultural, and recreational opportunities. The *Standards* highlight the need for:

- opportunities to develop greater internal strength and personal health;

- observation and interaction with positive adult role models;

- opportunities to participate in community service programs; and

- accessible recreational and other leisure time activities.[109]

Although limited data is available, studies suggest that youths leaving out-of-home care at age 18 often lack services such as legal assistance and social, cultural, and recreational opportunities. In a Westat study, only 10 percent of the youths received services to enhance their ability to access legal services.[110] The need for legal services after discharge was explored only in terms of involvement with the criminal justice system. In its follow-up study, Westat learned that 25 percent of the youths had experienced problems with the law since discharge.[111] Of those young people, 51 percent reported that drugs or alcohol use was involved in their legal problems.[112]

Member agencies responding to the CWLA survey described a variety of ways in which they strive to meet the needs of youths, including recreational activities such as field trips to cultural events, camp retreats, and picnics (56 percent); mentoring programs in which youths are paired with adults who serve as role models (6 percent); and referral to community resources to address social, cultural, and recreational needs (20 percent). With regard to legal services, 30 percent of the responding agencies provided clients with information on community resources that provide legal assistance, assistance in reading legal documents, and education regarding the legal rights and responsibilities of youths. Thirteen percent of the agencies stated that they refer clients to legal resources in the community.

Summary

Research focusing on the service needs of youths in out-of-home care, best practice standards, and information from youth-serving agencies provide insight into the direction that programs should take in developing and strengthening the ability of youths in care to live as independent and self-sufficient adults. In order to assist youths to develop into productive adults, caseworkers, foster parents, and child care workers must be able to identify and respond to the specific needs of youths as they begin to prepare for and make the transition into an independent living situation; must be trained to engage youths constructively and empower them to fully develop their own abilities and strengths; and must have the skills needed to support the transition to and maintenance of self-sufficiency by the youth. Independent living programs must incorporate a focus on education, job training, and employment experiences for youths; preparation in basic living skills; family involvement; health care services; and the development of community resources, housing, and aftercare support systems that begin before the youth leaves out-of-home care and continue after discharge. While many agencies recognize the need for these services and provide them to the extent their resources allow, much more needs to be done to ensure that youths are prepared to meet the challenges they will face as they become adults.

Notes

1.   Toshio Tatara, *Characteristics of Children in Substitute and Adoptive Care: A Statistical Summary of the VCIS National Child Welfare Data Base* (Washington, DC: American Public Welfare Association, March 1992), 83 (hereafter Tatara 1992). Recent data suggest the number may be even higher. See, for example, D. Bass, *Helping Vulnerable Youths: Runaway and Homeless Adolescents in the United States* (Washington, DC: NASW Press 1992), 2–12; R. Barth, "On Their Own: The Experience of Youth After Foster Care," *Child and Adolescent Social Work* 7, 5 (October 1990): 419.

2.   National Commission on Children, *Beyond Rhetoric* (Washington, DC: National Commission on Children, 1991), 284.

3.   Westat, Inc., *A National Evaluation of Title IV-E Foster Care Independent Living Programs for Youth*, Phase I, Final Report (Rockville, MD: Westat, Inc., 1988), vol. 1: 4-3 (hereafter Westat 1988). The national study of youths leaving foster care and independent living programs conducted by Westat, Inc. that is relied upon in this monograph examined the case histories and family backgrounds of 1,650 youth ages 16 years and older who were discharged from out-of-home care between January 1, 1987 and July 31, 1988, in an attempt to identify the characteristics of the national total of 34,600 youth discharged from care during the same time period. While some have criticized the study's methodology, the study does provide the most extensive and, in many instances, the only data available in this area. Two reports emerged from this study: a 1988 report that reviews the characteristics of youths in out-of-home care and their families and the types of independent living programs serving them, and a 1991 report that utilizes the data set forth in the 1988 report and advances recommendations on the basis of those findings. Both reports are cited throughout this monograph.

4.   E.V. Mech, "Preparing Foster Adolescents for Self-Support: A New Challenge for Child Welfare Services, " in *Independent Living Services for At-Risk Adolescents,* edited by Edmund V. Mech (Washington, DC: Child Welfare League of America,

1988), 489 (hereiafter Mech 1988). The book was originally published as a special issue of *Child Welfare* (vol. LXVII, no. 6, November–December 1988).

5. Westat 1988, 1: 4–5.

6. Westat 1988, 1: 3–4.

7. Tatara 1992, 61–63. The ages for some children were not recorded.

8. Tatara 1992, 76–77.

9. Westat 1988, 1: 4–13.

10. Westat 1988, 1: 4–14.

11. Westat, Inc., *A National Evaluation of Title IV-E Foster Care Independent Living Programs for Youth,* Phase 2, Final Report (Rockville, MD: Westat, Inc., 1991), vol. 1: 4–10 (hereafter Westat 1991).

12. H.C. Hornby and M.I. Collins, "Teenagers in Foster Care: The Forgotten Majority." *Children and Youth Services Review* 3, 1 and 2 (1981): 7–20.

13. Westat 1991, 1: 4–36.

14. Westat 1991, 1: 4–36.

15. Westat 1991, 1: 4–36.

16. Westat 1991, 1: 4–36.

17. Westat 1988, 1: 4–16.

18. Westat 1988, 1: 4–16.

19. Bass 1992, 2.

20. Bass 1992, 5.

21. Bass 1992, 5.

22. Westat 1988, 1: 4–20.

23. Westat 1988, 1: 4–36.

24. Bass 1992, 9.

25. T. Festinger, *No One Ever Asked Us: A Postscript to Foster Care* (New York: Columbia University Press, 1983).

26. Mech 1988: xiv.

27. Child Welfare League of America, *Standards for Independent Living Services* (Washington, DC: Child Welfare League of America, 1989), §2.2.

28. *CWLA Standards for Independent Living Services* §2.3.

29. *CWLA Standards for Independent Living Services* §2.4.

30. *CWLA Standards for Independent Living Services* §2.5.

31. *CWLA Standards for Independent Living Services* §2.6.

32. *CWLA Standards for Independent Living Services* §2.8.

33. *CWLA Standards for Independent Living Services* §2.8.

34. *CWLA Standards for Independent Living Services* §2.9.

35. *CWLA Standards for Independent Living Services* §2.3.

36. Nathan Weber, *Independent Youth Development Organizations: An Exploratory Study*. Unpublished paper prepared for the Carnegie Council on Adolescent Development, Task Force on Youth Development and Community Programs, May 1992: 36 (hereafter Carnegie 1992).

37. Westat 1991, 1: xiii, 3–14.

38. R. Cook, and D. Ansell, *Study of Independent Living Services for Youth in Substitute Care* (Rockville, MD: Westat, Inc., 1986).

39. Westat 1991, 1: 1–6.

40. Westat 1991, 1: 1–6.

41. Ohio Department of Human Services, *Children in Out-of-Home Care* (Columbus, OH: Division of Children and Family Services, 1987).

42. Westat 1988, 1: 4–17 to 4–19.

43. Westat, 1988, 1: 4–18.

44. Westat 1988, 1: 4–23.

45. Westat 1988, 1: 4–17; Westat 1991, 1: xiv, xv.

46. Westat 1991, 1: xv.

47. Festinger 1983.

48. *CWLA Standards for Independent Living Services* §2.4.

49. Westat 1988, 1: 4–21.

50. Westat 1988, 1: 4–23.

51. Westat 1991, 1: 3–12.

52. Westat 1991, 1: xv.

53. *CWLA Standards for Independent Living Services* §4.10.

54. *CWLA Standards for Independent Living Services* §4.11.

55. *CWLA Standards for Independent Living Services* §4.14.

56. *CWLA Standards for Independent Living Services* §4.15.

57. *CWLA Standards for Independent Living Services* §4.16.

58. *CWLA Standards for Independent Living Services* §4.17.

59. *CWLA Standards for Independent Living Services* §2.2.

60. Westat 1988, 1: 4–21, 4-22; Festinger 1984.

61. R. Barth, "On Their Own: The Experience of Youth After Foster Care," *Child and Adolescent Social Work* 7, 5 (October 1990): 426 (hereafter Barth 1990).

62. Westat 1988, 1: 4–21.

63. Adapted from Westat 1988, 1: 4–23.

64. *CWLA Standards for Independent Living Services* §0.4, §3.21

65. *CWLA Standards for Independent Living Services* §0.4.

66. Westat 1988, 1: 4–13 to 4–14.

67. Westat 1988, 1: 4–13 to 4–15.

68. Carnegie 1992, 36.

69. *CWLA Standards for Independent Living Services* §2.5.

70. *CWLA Standards for Independent Living Services* §4.12.

71. Child Welfare League of America, *Standards for Health Care Services for Children in Out-of-Home Care* (Washington, DC: Child Welfare League of America, 1988), §3.8.

72. *CWLA Standards for Independent Living Services* §4.12.

73. *CWLA Standards for Independent Living Services* §4.13.

74. Westat 1988, 1: 4–23.

75. Barth 1990, 429.

76. Barth 1990, 429.

77. CWLA North American Commission on Chemical Dependency and Child Welfare, *Children at the Front: A Different View of the War on Alcohol and Drugs* (Washington, DC: Child Welfare League of America, 1992), 38.

78. Select Committee on Children, Youth and Families, House of Representatives, 102nd Cong., 1st Sess., "The Risky Business of Adolescence: How to Help Teens Stay Safe" (Parts 1 and 2) (June 17, 1991) (Washington, D.C.: U.S. Government Printing Office, 1992): 4, *citing* National Institute for Drug Abuse, 1990 (hereafter "Risky Business").

79. "Risky Business" 1991, (Part 1): 4 *citing* National Institute for Drug Abuse, 1990.

80. "Risky Business" 1991 (Part 1): 4, *citing* U.S. Department of Health and Human Services, 1991.

81. The Center for Population Options, "The Role of Alcohol and Drug Abuse on Adolescent HIV Transmission," *Options* (Fall/Winter 1991): 3 (hereafter *Options* 1991).

82. "Risky Business" 1991 (Part 2): 31 *citing* the Centers for Disease Control, HIV/ AIDS Surveillance Report, July 1989 and February 1991.

83. "Risky Business" 1991 (Part 1), *citing* the Centers for Disease Control, 1991.

84. Report of the Presidential Commission on the Human Immunodeficiency Virus Epidemic (Washington, DC: U.S. Government Printing Office, 1991).

85. L.J. D'Angelo, P.R. Geston, C. O. Brasseux, M.F. Guagliardo, and N. Shaffer, *A Longitudinal Study of HIV Infection in Urban Adolescents*. (Washington, DC: Children's National Medical Center, and Atlanta, GA: Centers for Disease Control, 1991).

86. Barth 1990, 426–27.

87. Westat 1991, 1: 3–20.

88. Westat 1991, 1: 3–20.

89. Westat 1991, 1: xv.

90. Select Committee on Children, Youth and Families, House of Representatives, 102nd Cong., 2d Sess. *A Decade of Denial: Teens and AIDS in America* (Washington, DC: U.S. Government Printing Office, 1992), xviii (hereafter "A Decade of Denial").

91. "Risky Business" 1991 (Part 1): 5 *citing* U.S. Department of Health and Human Services, 1990; Darroch, Forrest and Singh, 1990; Sonenstein, 1989.

92. "Risky Business," 1991 (Part 1): 4, *citing* U.S. Department of Health and Human Services, 1990; National Center for Health Statistics, 1990.

93. "Risky Business," 1991 (Part 1): 5, *citing* Moster, 1990; Darroch, Forrest, and Singh, 1990; Sonenstein, 1989.

94. T. Ooms and T. Owen, "Promoting Adolescent Health and Well Being through

School-Linked, Multi-Service, Family Friendly Programs," *Background Briefing Report and Meeting Highlights* (Washington, DC: The American Association of Marriage and Family Therapists Research and Education Foundation, 1991), 4.

95. *Options* 1991.

96. *CWLA Standards for Independent Living Services* §2.9.

97. *CWLA Standards for Independent Living Services* §0.5.

98. Westat 1988, 1: 4–24.

99. J. Duva and G. Raley, *Transitional Difficulties of Out-of-Home Youth* (Washington, DC: Youth and America's Future: The William T. Grant Foundation Commission on Work, Family, and Citizenship, 1988).

100. *CWLA Standards for Independent Living Services* §2.6.

101. *CWLA Standards for Independent Living Services* § 4.15.

102. Westat 1988, 1: 4–23.

103. Westat, Inc., *Independent Living Services for Youth in Substitute Care* (Washington, DC: Administration for Children and Youth, June 1986), 6–11.

104. Ibid, 6–12.

105. Westat 1991, 1: 4–10.

106. Westat 1991, 1: 4–11.

107. Westat 1991, 1: 4–11.

108. *CWLA Standards for Independent Living Services* §2.7.

109. *CWLA Standards for Independent Living Services* §2.8.

110. Westat, Inc., *A National Evaluation of Title IV-E Foster Care Independent Living Programs for Youth,* Phase 1, Final Report (Washington, DC: U.S. Department of Health and Human Services, 1988), vol. 1: 4–23.

111. Westat, Inc., *A National Evaluation of Title IV-E Foster Care Independent Living Programs for Youth,* Phase 2, Final Report (Washington, DC: U.S. Department of Health and Human Services, 1991), vol. 1: 4–25.

112. Westat 1988, 1: 4–25.

SECTION II:

The Federal Independent Living Program

The federal Independent Living Program[1] under Title IV-E of the Social Security Act is designed to provide all states with funds to assist youths in out-of-home care prepare for self-sufficiency and independence as adults. Opinions vary widely, however, as to the extent to which the program actually provides the level of support needed for independent living services.

In many areas of the country, public and voluntary child welfare agencies have effectively used Title IV-E Independent Living Program funds to develop a heightened capacity to prepare youths who are discharged from the child welfare system with the basic living skills, education, and employment preparation they will need to survive. These agencies view the federal funds as an important resource that has supported the development and implementation of quality independent living services. Other agencies, however, have had difficulty providing youths with the level of preparation they need, despite the availability of funds under the program. These agencies cite limited resources, eligibility restrictions, lack of coordination with other programs and the community, and the emotional and behavioral problems that many youths suffer because of abuse, neglect, and the lack of a permanent home. For some of these agencies, the federal Independent Living Program has not offered the resources necessary to develop comprehensive independent living programs for youths in out-of-home care.

These differing experiences with the federal Independent Living Program have given rise to many questions about the program—the scope of the services funded, the resources the program offers to agencies that seek to provide independent living services, the barriers to service that have not been adequately addressed, and the extent to which communities have been able to use the program to offer youths the range of essential independent living services.

Program History

Prior to the enactment of the federal Independent Living Program, most child welfare agencies did not offer specific services to adolescents to prepare them for independence. Less than half of the states had written policies that described the services that youths should receive before discharge from out-of-home care.[2]

The landmark Child Welfare and Adoption Assistance Act of 1980[3] also had overlooked the specific needs of these youths. Its intent was to restructure the nation's out-of-home care system to prevent the unnecessary placement of children and youths in care and to move youngsters from temporary placements into permanent families in a timely manner. It did not, however, address the needs of those youths who were likely to remain in out-of-home care on a long-term basis, graduating from out-of-home care to independence at age 18.

In 1984, U.S. Senator Daniel Patrick Moynihan, with U.S. Representative Fortney Stark, introduced legislation to create the federal Independent Living Program. At hearings convened by the House Ways and Means and Senate Finance Committees in 1984 and 1985, CWLA urged passage of the legislation, testifying that in many states, youths who did not return to their families of origin and who were not adopted were effectively on their own once they left out-of-home care. Congress learned that youths discharged from out-of-home care at age 18 often experienced substantial difficulties and faced, in greater numbers than youths who had never lived in out-of-home care, homelessness, arrests for serious crimes, and dependence on Aid to Families with Dependent Children and other forms of public assistance.[4]

In 1986, with the strong support of CWLA and its member agencies, Congress passed the Independent Living Program legislation as part of a massive budget bill, the Consolidated Omnibus Budget Reconciliation Act. Congress provided the program with $45 million,[5] but the Reagan Administration balked at implementing the new program. Although the statute specifically directed the U.S. Department of Health and Human Services (HHS) to issue regulations and award funds within 60 days of the bill's April 1986 enactment, HHS did not inform states of the program's existence until February 1987, fully 10 months after the bill was signed into law. After the failure of Administration attempts to repeal the legislation and divert the funds to other programs, HHS provided states with their initial allotments for the program in the summer of 1987 and program implementation began.[6]

Despite its somewhat tenuous beginning, the federal Independent Living Program has grown steadily. The funding, dedicated specifically to meeting adolescents' needs, has enabled states to implement or expand programs to assist youths in making the transition from out-of-home care to self-sufficiency. Currently, all 50 states and the District of Columbia provide some independent living services to youths.[7] Prior to August 10, 1993, when President Clinton signed the Omnibus Budget Reconciliation Act (OBRA) of 1993, the federal Independent Living Program did not have permanent program status. States had been required to depend on Congressional reauthorization of the program and many had hesitated to expand their commitment of resources and personnel to independent living programs, fearing they would not receive federal assistance in the foreseeable future. With the permanent authorization of the program by OBRA 1993, it is anticipated that states will consider broader implementation of independent living programs.

Program Overview

The federal Independent Living Program is designed for youths in out-of-home care who will neither return to their families nor be adopted and for whom out-of-home care has become a permanent situation until they age out of care. Independent living services may be made available to youths beginning at age 16 and continue through age 18, or at state option, through age 21. Because eligibility for independent living services is not limited to youths who are Title IV-E eligible,[8] all adolescents in out-of-home care may receive services funded through the federal Independent Living Program. Virginia is the only state to limit eligibility for independent living services to youths who are eligible for Title IV-E foster care maintenance payments.

A range of independent living services may be funded under the federal program, including instruction in the basics of daily living such as housekeeping, money management, and nutrition; assistance in finishing high school and preparing for college; employment preparation, including job training or placement or personal presentation and social skills; and individual and group counseling. Wide flexibility is permitted within these parameters to design and implement independent living programs. States, counties, and cities may operate their own independent living programs or governmental entities may contract with voluntary agencies to provide independent living services.

The federal Independent Living Program currently receives a total annual appropriation of $70 million. The government distributes these funds to states through a formula based on the percentage of children in the state who received federal foster care assistance in 1984, the most recent year for which data were available when the Independent Living Program was established in 1986. States are required to match, dollar-for-dollar, any amount they receive over their portion of the original $45 million allotment available in 1986. HHS reallocates to states that request additional federal resources any funds remaining from allotments to states that cannot make use of the entire federal match.

Table two, based on federal Independent Living Initiative State Program Plans for Fiscal Year 1992,[9] provides a state-by-state breakdown of the use of the expanded eligibility option to age 21, the number of eligible youths who will receive independent living services, the state's base level of funding, and the extent to which the state has taken advantage of additional federal funds.

Implementation of the Program

Evidence from the Westat studies suggests that the federal Independent Living Program has encouraged states to pay greater attention to youths' needs. Increasingly, states have applied program funds to expand

Table Two
The Independent Living Program under Title IV-E
(Based on FY92 Independent Living Initiative State Program Plans)

State	Does the state serve youths up to age 21?	# of youths expected to be in care in FY92	# of youths expected to be served in FY92	Base federal funding amount FY93	Additional federal funds (to be matched) FY93	Total federal allotment FY93*
Alabama	yes	862	750	$667,601	$370,889	$1,038,490
Alaska	yes	326	60	8,378	4,654	13,032
Arizona	no	450	260	223,562	124,201	347,763
Arkansas	yes	364	270	174,176	96,764	270,940
California	county option	18,203	13,960	8,023,999	4,457,778	12,481,777
Colorado	yes	1,611	1,280	530,906	294,948	825,854
Connecticut	yes	732	350	485,047	269,471	754,518
Delaware	yes	300	165	130,522	72,512	203,034
Dist. of Col.	yes	441	110	701,995	389,997	1,091,992
Florida	yes	2,275	1,328	634,529	352,516	987,045
Georgia	yes	1,733	1,356	706,405	392,447	1,098,852
Hawaii	no	200	50	11,465	6,369	17,834
Idaho	yes	337	204	68,788	38,216	107,004
Illinois	yes	3,675	2,427	1,810,989	1,006,105	2,817,094
Indiana	yes	1,430	715	655,695	364,275	1,019,970
Iowa	yes	1,430	1,430	289,264	160,702	449,966

continued...

TABLE TWO (CONTINUED)

State	Does the state serve youths up to age 21?	# of youths expected to be in care in FY92	# of youths expected to be served in FY92	Base federal funding amount FY93	Additional federal funds (to be matched) FY93	Total federal allotment FY93*
Kansas	no	1,492	1,492	461,235	256,242	717,477
Kentucky	no	1,500	500	508,858	282,699	791,557
Louisiana	yes	266	190	873,084	485,047	1,358,131
Maine	yes	675	194	363,785	202,103	565,888
Maryland	no	1,409	1,150	795,918	442,177	1,238,095
Massachusetts	yes	2,513	450	408,762	227,090	635,852
Michigan	yes	4,908	3000	2,681,869	1,489,927	4,171,796
Minnesota	no	4,000	1,200	734,185	407,881	1,142,066
Mississippi	yes	594	301	330,714	183,730	514,444
Missouri	yes	1,123	619	832,517	462,509	1,295,026
Montana	yes	406	203	156,979	87,211	244,190
Nebraska	yes	988	950	280,004	155,558	435,562
Nevada	yes	414	182	98,773	54,874	153,647
New Hampshire	no	500 - 600	300 - 350	205,924	114,402	320,326
New Jersey	yes	1,500	500	1,477,188	820,660	2,297,848
New Mexico	no	266	190	133,167	73,982	207,149
New York	yes	8,500	6,073	7,448,116	4,137,842	11,585,958
North Carolina	yes	967	967	672,010	373,339	1,045,349
North Dakota	yes	220	220	123,466	68,592	192,058

Ohio	yes	3,616	3,616	1,839,209	1,021,783	2,860,992
Oklahoma	yes	517	517	398,620	221,456	620,076
Oregon	yes	2600	1500	598,371	332,428	930,799
Pennsylvania	yes	4,800	1,500	2,981,716	1,656,509	4,638,225
Rhode Island	yes	781	279	202,397	122,443	314,840
South Carolina	yes	524	498	372,604	207,002	579,606
South Dakota	yes	90	90	124,348	69,082	193,430
Tennessee	yes	1,685	819	500,039	277,799	777,838
Texas	yes	1,368	1,343	1,183,955	657,753	1,841,708
Utah	no	479	250	130,081	72,267	202,348
Vermont	yes	404	270	190,050	105,583	295,633
Virginia	yes	1,430	715	875,289	486,272	1,361,561
Washington	yes	1,300	400	530,465	294,703	825,168
West Virginia	yes	1,084	611	335,123	186,179	521,302
Wisconsin	yes	1,800	900	999,196	555,109	1,554,305
Wyoming	yes	65	38	28,662	15,923	44,585

*   This information is based on FY92 Independent Living Initiative State Program Plans, U.S. Department of Health and Human Services, Administration for Children and Families; and Administration for Children, Youth and Families, U.S. Department of Health and Human Services, Log No. ACYF-PI-93-01 (Issuance Date: 01-15-93). Six states did not accept the full federal matching fund amount. These were: District of Columbia (turned back $389,997); Louisiana (turned back $285,047); Michigan (turned back $289,927); Tennessee (turned back $147,619); Virginia (turned back $486,272); and West Virginia (turned back $186,179). Source: U.S. Department of Health and Human Services, Administration for Children and Families.

and enhance existing independent living programs and have utilized the leeway the law gives states to tailor independent living services to meet the specific needs of their client populations. For example, before the enactment of the Independent Living Program, only half of the states offered basic skills training classes for youths; all states now provide this instruction. Community outreach and interagency planning also have improved. Advisory councils now operate in 21 states, as compared to only six states prior to enactment of the law. The use of formal interagency agreements has likewise expanded: such agreements have now been implemented in 20 states as compared to only eight states prior to enactment of the law.[10]

On the other hand, the federal Independent Living Program, despite its successes, has not provided a definitive solution to the difficulties many communities encounter in attempting to develop and implement comprehensive independent living programs. Implementation of the program has been uneven across the country, a situation often attributed to a lack of consistent federal guidance and oversight, inadequate state human service budgets, and, in some states, a reluctance to deal with the special needs of youths.

There is considerable variation in the services that states provide to prepare adolescents for life on their own. Similarity exists in the basic range of services identified under federal law: education and/or employment assistance, training in daily living skills, individual and group counseling, integration and coordination of services, outreach, and a written transitional independent living plan for each participant. Table three identifies the independent living services offered by each state, based on the Independent Living Initiative State Program Plans submitted by the states for Fiscal Year 1992 to the U.S. Department of Health and Human Services.

States report that their independent living programs serve youths from a number of service systems. In many states, youths enter independent living primarily from child welfare settings, such as family foster care, residential treatment facilities, group homes, and emergency shelters. In other states, referrals come from both the child welfare and the juvenile justice systems. In these states, multiple funding streams support independent living programs for youths, with funds from the Runaway and Homeless Youth Act and state appropriations supplementing independent living funds under Title IV-E. Some states also extend independent living

TABLE THREE

Independent Living Services Provided by States

(Based on FY92 Independent Living Initiative State Program Plans)

State	Offers All Basic Services*	Offers Additional Optional Services
Alabama	✓	assessment; teen conference; newsletter; teen advisory board; teen parenting; mentors; stipends; evaluation
Alaska	✓	training for foster care providers
Arizona	✓	training for foster parents and child care providers; cash incentives for youths with saving accounts and who complete high school or GED
Arkansas	✓	post-discharge services of youth's options; newspaper; getting ready
California	✓	independent-living training for foster parents; independent living case management for social workers and group home staff
Colorado	✓	evaluation; staff/foster parent training; newsletter; conference assessment; database; sex education; teen parenting; stipends
Connecticut	✓	trust funds
Delaware	✓	independent living Advisory Board/Department Advisory Committee; annual teen conference; specialized training for foster parents
Dist. of Columbia	✓	college tuition for six youths
Florida	✓	training; assessment; mentoring; conference; tutoring; stipends; teen parenting; accessing resources
Georgia	✓	assessment; staff/foster parent training; data collection; aftercare; conference; preparing/presenting AIDS video/drama project; scholarships; newsletter; mentoring
Hawaii	**	teen conference; mentor program
Idaho	✓	training for staff/foster care providers

continued...

TABLE THREE (CONTINUED)

State	Offers All Basic Services*	Offers Additional Optional Services
Illinois	✓	relative involvement; community care management model; trust funds; $500 stipend
Indiana	✓	none reported
Iowa	✓	foster parent independent-living services training
Kansas	✓	six months aftercare
Kentucky	✓	special staff training; stipends; mentors teen conferences
Louisiana	✓	specialized training for foster parents and child care providers
Maine	✓	teen conference
Maryland	✓	trust funds
Massachusetts	✓	local banks teach youths how to use services; schools provide program for deaf
Michigan	✓	clinical services to focus on social interaction, conflict resolution, problem solving and relationship
Minnesota	✓	training for social service staff/foster parents/volunteers
Mississippi	✓	conference; foster parent/worker training; stipend; six months aftercare
Missouri	✓	newsletter; stipends; driver's education
Montana	✓	stipends; mentors; technical assistance to case managers; training; tutors; evaluation; linkages; involve relatives
Nebraska	✓	none reported
Nevada	✓	staff/foster parent training; emancipation support; teen conference
New Hampshire	✓	none reported
New Jersey	✓	six months aftercare
New Mexico	✓	none reported
New York	✓	stipends; aftercare; independent living resource network

State		Services
North Carolina	✓	relative involvement
North Dakota	✓	statewide policies/database; evaluation; technical; assistance and foster parent/staff training; conference; stipends; transitional living; tracker program
Ohio	**	support services for teen moms; school curriculum for "at risk populations"
Oklahoma	✓	none reported
Oregon	✓	staff/foster parent training
Pennsylvania	✓	stipends; ongoing support networks for discharged youth; self-esteem; aid to teen and parents
Rhode Island	✓	newsletter; Youth Advisory Committee
South Carolina	**	leadership development; conference; staff/foster parent training; program standards; newsletter
South Dakota	✓	assessment; mentors; staff foster parent training; stipends; tracking; conference
Tennessee	✓	staff/foster parent training; evaluation; resource access; directory; mentors; newsletter; conference; therapeutic foster homes
Texas	✓	statewide teen conference; mentor programs; purchase of legal services for youths
Utah	✓	staff/foster parent training; independent living committee; management information; data collection; teen conference
Vermont	✓	teen conference; Teen Advisory Board
Virginia	✓	linkages with community
Washington	✓	training for staff, contractors and foster care providers; research on effectiveness; trust funds
West Virginia	✓	none reported
Wisconsin	✓	none reported
Wyoming	✓	health; aftercare; staff training

*   Basic services are: education and/or employment assistance; training in daily living skills; individual and group counseling; integration and coordination or services; outreach; and a written transitional individual living plan for each participant.

** Hawaii offers selected basic services, including education/employment, daily living skills, outreach, and a written plan. Ohio and South Carolina offer selected basic services, including education/employment, daily living skills, coordination of services, and a written plan.

services to youths with disabilities who are not likely to be able to live on their own.

Little information is available to permit an evaluation of the outcomes achieved as a result of providing independent living services to youths. State plans reflect the services that states provide but they do not assess the quality or intensity of services provided or the extent to which various approaches prepare youths to live independently after discharge from out-of-home care. Michigan and Washington, however, are currently conducting longitudinal studies to assess the effectiveness of the independent living services they provide.

Notes

1. 42 U.S.C.A. §677.

2. Westat, Inc., *A National Evaluation of Title IV-E Foster Care Independent Living Programs for Youth,* Phase 2, Final Report (Rockville, MD: Westat, Inc., 1991), vol. 1: 1–6 (hereafter Westat 1991).

3. 42 U.S.C. Section §§670–679.

4. M. Allen, K. Bonner, and L. Greenan, "Federal Legislative Support for Independent Living." *In Independent Living Services for At-Risk Adolescents* (Washington, DC: Child Welfare League of America, Inc., 1988) (hereafter Allen 1988), 20.

5. Allen 1988, 20.

6. Allen 1988, 23–24.

7. Westat 1991, 1: 1–6.

8. Title IV-E eligibility requires that the child or youth (1) be eligible for Aid to Families with Dependent Children (AFDC); and (2) be placed in out-of-home care based on a judicial determination that continuation in the home would be contrary to the child's or youth's best interest.

9. Independent Living Initiative State Program Plans must be submitted annually by each state participating in the federal program.

10. Westat 1991, 1: 1–6.

SECTION III

Three Examples of Independent-Living Programs

Of the many agencies with excellent independent living programs that responded to the 1992 CWLA survey, three were selected to illustrate the range of independent living services. These programs contain elements that other programs might consider when planning and implementing independent living programs and designing effective service plans to assist youths in making the transition from out-of-home care to independent living. The descriptions are provided not as "models" but as examples of diverse approaches that can spark creative thinking among professionals committed to improving the lives of youths and assisting them in their transition from out-of-home care to self-sufficient adulthood.

The Connecticut Program

The state of Connecticut operates an independent living program for youths up to age 21 living in family foster care, group care, residential care, or emergency shelters. Connecticut's program is divided into four major components to meet the needs of youths in different out-of-home care settings.

Component I: The Community Life Skills Project

Connecticut's Community Life Skills project consists of 12 projects for youths age 16 and older living in out-of-home care. The average Community Life Skills participant is 16½, lives in a relative's home, and has been in care for five years or more. The projects involve youths, primary caregivers, and mentors, and provide academic instruction, daily living skills training, vocational education, and career preparation. Youths in the Community Life Skills Project are awarded a stipend of $300 to $500 for successful completion of the program. Success is defined as 85% attendance and participation in the program activities.

Component II: Preparation for Adult Living Settings

Connecticut's second program component provides staff-supervised individual apartment living for youths currently residing in residential care who, though not yet ready for living independently in the community, are ready to live in a less restrictive setting. Managed as a collaboration between the Connecticut Association of Residential Facilities and the Connecticut Department of Youth Services, this program offers three state-funded transitional living sites for youths in out-of-home care. Federal Independent Living program funds under Title IV-E are used to develop individual case plans and provide training in daily living skills and vocational and academic assessment.

Component III: Community Housing Assistance

Connecticut's third program component, Community Housing Assistance, is designed for youths who have exhibited the skills and competencies needed to leave out-of-home care and reside in community housing with a minimum of supervision and services. Staff members assist youths in establishing community housing and offer services such as assistance in developing monthly budgets that cover rent, food, utilities, telephone service, transportation, and miscellaneous expenses. Participants contribute half of their net earned income toward their expenses; the remainder is deposited in a personal savings account. Project goals include locating and maintaining appropriate housing, building a "nest egg" of personal savings, finding employment in a marketable field, accessing community and social resources, and developing self-reliance and personal skills.

Component IV: Aftercare

The final component of Connecticut's program assists youths who have completed the above components and are on their own. Although not completely operational at present, this component is designed as a time-limited service that will offer supportive and referral services for youths after they make the transition to independence. The goal is to have each young adult form a relationship with a case manager who can then act as an additional safety net as the youth continues to develop self-sufficiency.

Summary

While Connecticut's program implementation has been successful, it is not problem-free. In addition to such common problems as lack of funds, an insufficient number of caseworkers trained in the special problems of adolescents, and difficulties in program coordination, the program serves a diverse group of clients (each of whom require a different mix and intensity of services): youths with stable placements in family foster care, youths who have had multiple placements in out-of-home care, youths with multiple disabilities, and youths who are chemically dependent. At times, community-based programs have been reluctant to serve adolescents in general, and to serve youths with multiple problems who are in out-of-home care. In addition, unavoidable program barriers may discourage youths, such as a waiting period to participate in the program and the need to obtain a birth certificate and other paperwork necessary to enroll in the program.

Minnesota's "Support for Emancipation and Living Functionally" (SELF) Program

Minnesota's SELF program draws its participants from family foster care, group homes, residential treatment facilities, biological families and relatives, emergency shelters, correctional facilities, and youths living on their own. Supported primarily through federal Title IV-E Independent Living funds, the program is county-administered and implemented by public agencies and by private, nonprofit agencies who receive contracts to develop innovative programs accessible to county social service agencies. Voluntary agency grantees are selected with the goal of achieving diversity in agency size, service specialty, geographic location, and type of program. County social service staff refer clients to grantee programs.

The program is based on a life-skills training plan. Participants receive individual and group instruction by public and private agency staff, and services are coordinated among state and federal programs and community resources. Services include assistance in budgeting; locating and maintaining housing; accessing health care services; job training, placement, and career counseling; preparing for high school graduation and admission to college; improving social skills and increasing self-esteem; drivers' education; and English as a Second Language instruction. Incentive payments, such as stipends for participation in the program, matched savings, and goods purchased with SELF funds (including YMCA memberships, music lessons, household goods, transportation costs, driver's permits or license fees, tuition, books, and tools for vocational programs) are also available.

A recently established $400,000 grant pool has allowed Minnesota to further expand its program, including the development of a rural training program, the establishment of a week-long residential urban survival program, the provision of support stipends for public transportation, the development of an Independent Living program for Native American youths, and the recruitment and training of "emancipation foster homes."

Cincinnati's New Life Youth Services

New Life Youth Services in Cincinnati, Ohio is a private, nonprofit agency that serves, at any time, 20 to 30 clients between the ages of 16 and 20. These clients, who enter the New Life Youth Services' program following discharge from family foster care, group homes, residential treatment, or correctional institutions, rent privately-owned apartments in the Cincinnati area. They are provided with housing support and training to prepare them for life on their own.

Services begin with a focus on housing. A social worker and the youth work together to find an apartment that best meets the needs of the youth. New Life Youth Services staff supervise the youth while he or she is living in the apartment, and landlords are assured that the program will pay for rent, utilities, telephone service, furniture, and any damage to the property. Each youth participant must do volunteer work, attend school, or hold a job for at least 20 hours each week.

Clients receive training in daily living skills, including the purchase of groceries and preparation of nutritious meals; participate in an individualized, 24-session life-skills training course; and attend regular workshops, recreational activities, and weekly group sessions on self-sufficiency preparation. Every youth receives a weekly stipend of $55. Of this amount, $10 is deposited into the participant's savings account. The remainder of the allowance is used for groceries, transportation, household items, and miscellaneous expenses.

The New Life Youth Services program emphasizes individualized attention. Participants are enrolled for a minimum of three months to a maximum of two years; throughout that period, they receive ongoing case management, counseling, and support services. The program also makes use of volunteer mentors, and operates a 24-hour hotline that connects a youth to a social worker if problems arise.

The program defines the "successful" participant as one who has obtained a high school degree or its equivalent, maintained a full-time job, accrued savings, and demonstrated that he or she has acquired the other skills necessary to live independently. If a participant meets the above conditions, he or she "graduates," but can maintain residence in the apartment. Between 25 and 30 percent of clients successfully complete the program, and more than 85 percent are employed at some point during participation in the program.

The 1992 budget for New Life Youth Services was $300,000 and drew upon a range of funding sources: federal Title IV-E monies for staff training, state foster care funds, county funds, and private sources such as foundation and corporate grants, United Way, and the Community Chest. New Life Youth Services scattered-site approach generates relatively low overhead, since there is no need to purchase a facility, and no need for a large staff.

SECTION IV
Recommendations

The federal Independent Living Program has great potential to assist youths in successfully establishing themselves as adults. In some communities, the program has been fully utilized. In other communities, however, significant gaps continue to exist. A review of the CWLA survey responses suggests that many agencies have not been able to provide the array of independent living services that youths need.

In the CWLA survey, agencies were asked to identify "gaps, obstacles, and/or limitations in independent living programs that do not address common problems facing youths." The most frequently cited obstacle was lack of financial resources to operate programs. Budgeting constraints posed substantial barriers to recruiting and retaining a sufficient number of experienced staff, recruiting mentors, providing comprehensive services, maintaining services after discharge, providing services to youths younger than 16, and exercising the federal option that allows states to offer independent living services to youths up to age 21.

In addition to financial constraints, the gaps, obstacles, and limitations that agencies frequently identified include:

- shortage of affordable, livable housing for transitional living arrangements;

- eligibility restrictions under the federal Independent Living Program;

- inconsistent aftercare services;

- poor integration with the child welfare system and the community;

- absence of teen pregnancy, adolescent parenting, and substance abuse services;

- bureaucratic gridlock;

- limited availability of child care for the children of parenting adolescents;

- limitations in federal law, particularly "room and board" restrictions on federal Independent Living Program funds, that preclude agencies from funding housing arrangements;

- difficulties in obtaining state licenses to operate transitional living arrangements; and

- lack of community support, particularly insufficient coordination of resources across the child welfare and education systems, duplication of services, and the lack of community involvement in providing appropriate role models for youths.

Agencies advocated strongly for the full integration of independent living services into the array of child welfare services. To achieve such integration, agencies stated that the following steps needed to be taken:

1. Social workers should be educated about the importance of preparation for discharge from out-of-home care.

2. Foster parents should be involved in preparing youths for emancipation.

3. Greater attention should be given to cross-cultural issues, including preparing youths to handle racial discrimination and assisting youths who are refugees in obtaining culturally competent services.

4. Independent living services should be extended to all youths in the child welfare system, including those who are known to the child welfare system but who have not been separated from their families and those who may be reunified with their families but who can still profit from independent- living skills training.

Further development and implementation of independent living services must be based on the needs of youths in out-of-home care, the extent to which the federal Independent Living Program is currently meeting those needs, and the limits, obstacles, and gaps identified by youth-serving agencies based on their own experience in providing independent living services.

Program Development

Although a number of programs are providing a comprehensive range of independent living services, numerous gaps are evident. The following steps are recommended:

1.   Continue and expand experiential services and provide a comprehensive range of independent living services.

Providing a mix of services tailored to each youth's individual goals and incorporating the actual experience of living on one's own are two of the most effective means of assisting youths to make the transition to independent living. These approaches need further support and development.

2.   Enhance the involvement of the community and young people themselves in the planning and delivery of services.

To support the efforts of adolescents to make a successful transition from out-of-home care to adulthood, program designs must incorporate not only agency and community resources, but community members and young people themselves. Youth advisory groups can provide important information on the needs of young persons and the relative effectiveness of services. Community involvement in the preparation and support of youths is likewise essential to the success of services that have as their ultimate goal the achievement of self-sufficiency.

3.   Strengthen aftercare services.

The inability of agencies to provide adequate aftercare services frequently appears to be a barrier to effective independent living programs. Innovative approaches, such as the use of volunteer mentors to maintain contact with youths, need to be developed, shared, and practiced by agencies that provide services to youths after discharge from care.

4.   Improve services to at-risk youths.

Youths in care are, in most respects, no different from youths who have lived their lives in the confines of their family of origin. These young people are at greater risk, however, because of their history of abuse or neglect. Youth services must recognize that youths in out-of-home care are at particular risk of becoming pregnant or a parent, abusing drugs or alcohol, contracting HIV, becoming homeless, or engaging in criminal behavior. Service plans for youths must be developed with these considerations in mind.

5.   Expand housing resources for youths.

Transitional housing for emancipated youths is critically important, yet support for housing services is often difficult to access. Efforts must be made to develop funding resources to support such services and to develop a range of housing options as part of the independent living program.

6.   Identify alternative funding sources for youth services.

Agencies need assistance in creatively accessing multiple sources of funding for program development, including Title IV-E Independent Living funds, alternative federal funding sources, state funding, and foundation and corporate donors. Expertise in creative resource development must be made available to programs.

Training

Training focusing on the needs of youths for independent living services and the skills needed to work effectively with youths is essential to successful outcomes in independent living programs. The following steps are recommended:

1. *Provide basic, ongoing training to staff members on how to prepare youths for independent living.*

Staff members who are trained to work with adolescents and committed to this area of child welfare practice are essential to the success of adolescents in making the transition to independent living.

2. *Provide culturally competent training to staff members.*

Agencies that serve racially and culturally diverse populations are aware of the cross-cultural barriers that can arise between agency staff members and their clients. To enhance the ability of youths from racially and culturally diverse groups to use the services most effectively, agencies must employ bilingual staff and have access to resource materials and staff training on cultural and racial issues that affect youths.

3. *Involve foster parents, child and youth care workers, and biological parents in preparing youths for independent living.*

Foster parents and child and youth care workers must be viewed as independent living service providers, so that they, too, are able to assist youths in making the transition from out-of-home care to self-sufficient living. In addition, efforts should be made to include biological families in the preparation process as well. Over half of the adolescents in out-of-home care return to their biological families following discharge.

4. *Provide staff and foster parents with practical skills to assist them in helping youths deal with the challenges of living independently.*

Youths who participate in independent living programs need considerable support in preparing for and meeting the challenges of living independently. Staff and foster parents must be assisted to develop skills in working with youths preparing to make it on their own and after discharge. They particularly need skills in helping youths deal with the frustrations and challenges inherent in making the transition to adulthood.

State and Federal Advocacy

A number of legislative changes are indicated to enhance independent living services for youths, including:

1.   *Urge state legislatures to use expanded eligibility options under the Title IV-E program.* *

An overwhelming majority of states have already taken advantage of federal options to extend independent living eligibility to youths up to age 21 and to youths who do not meet the requirements for federal foster care maintenance payments. Campaigns must be mounted to encourage the remaining states to, at a minimum, provide transition assistance to the broadest population allowable under federal law.

2.   *Urge Congress to increase the total level of federal Independent Living Program funds from $70 million to $100 million.*

Enhanced funding is essential to ensuring the effectiveness of the federal Independent Living Program. An increase in federal support from the current level of $70 million annually to $100 million annually would greatly assist states in committing resources to ongoing independent living programs, expanding programs to reach more youths in care, hiring and training personnel, providing youths with individualized service plans, and strengthening aftercare services.

3.   *Allow a portion of new federal funds allotted to the federal independent living program to be used to provide housing search assistance, housing-related counseling, limited subsidies for transitional housing expenses, and room and board in adult-supervised group living programs.*

Although some public and private agencies are able to leverage state and private funds to support transitional living arrangements for youths, many others are not. Experience in living on one's own is vital to a successful transition from out-of-home care to adulthood. Financial resources must be made available to support a range of housing services.

4.   *Amend the current Title IV-E Foster Care and Adoption Assistance program to give states the option to continue foster care maintenance*

---

*   The following states should be urged to extend emancipation services to youths up to age 21: Arizona, California, Hawaii, Kansas, Kentucky, Maryland, Minnesota, New Hampshire, New Mexico, and Utah. Virginia should be urged to extend services to youths who do not qualify for federal foster care maintenance payments.

payments—and the Medicaid coverage that accompanies them—to youths up to their 21st birthdays.

A legislative change allowing expanded eligibility for foster care maintenance and Medicaid would not only encourage states to improve contact with and support for youths beyond the current legal limit of foster care at age 18, but would also facilitate youths' access to health care, a gap in current services.

5. *Contingent on a funding increase for the federal Independent Living Program, allow states the option of lowering the age of eligibility for independent living services.*

A majority of agencies surveyed by CWLA strongly recommended allowing youths in out-of-home care to begin participating in independent living services at age 14. Earlier initiation of services allows youths to begin incorporating skills that can be strengthened and enhanced later (particularly basic skill building, health care services, and social, cultural, and recreational services).

6. *Amend the language in the federal Independent Living Program legislation to require that case plans outline the steps being taken to help youths obtain a high school degree or its equivalent.*

Because a high school degree strongly predicts successful integration into the community, completion of high school or its equivalent should be specifically addressed in the case plan of each youth. The attainment of a high school diploma or equivalent should be supported through an array of social services designed to help participants complete their education and identify a support network for further assistance.

7. *Encourage states to develop special initiatives offering education and other support services to pregnant and parenting adolescents participating in the Independent Living program.*

Federal Independent Living Program funds and funds under other programs such as Title X of the Public Health Services Act are available to help pregnant and parenting youths. Attention must be directed to the magnitude of the needs of youths in out-of-home care for such services. State, county, and local agencies must be assisted to develop new and more effective prevention and service programs.

Research

To date, most information on independent living is anecdotal. Other than the Westat study, virtually no recent objective national data exist on the effectiveness of independent living services or on the experiences of youths discharged from out-of-home care. To meet the need for such information, the following steps should be taken:

1. *Conduct objective research on the outcomes for youths who have received independent living services as compared to youths who do not receive such services.*

Outcome-related research is invaluable to policymakers, youth advocates, administrators, and caseworkers in designing and implementing programs to meet the needs of youths. Additionally, the dearth of current data makes future planning difficult. Research that objectively assesses the outcomes for youths who receive independent living services as compared to those who do not would provide a source of information currently unavailable to policymakers and service providers.

2. *Establish a clearinghouse for resource sharing among independent living programs.*

While the enactment in 1986 of the federal Independent Living Program provided support for many programs across the country, it has not facilitated communication among these programs. In fact, a comprehensive directory of independent living programs across the nation does not exist. Successful independent living programs also have been developed in other countries and provide models that could be replicated in the United States. Establishing a clearinghouse for information on independent living and creating a central library that would provide access to the latest research on effective practice would facilitate the sharing of information on effective strategies and allow programs to better assist the youths in their care.

Conclusion

Although the federal Independent Living Program has proven to be an effective means of preparing some young people in out-of-home care to make the transition to adulthood, the program as currently designed does not address the full range of youth needs. Policies, programs, and practice must be developed so that each youth in out-of-home care will have a solid education, employment preparation, economic security, affordable and accessible housing, health care, and safe and nurturing relationships intended to last a lifetime. To achieve that goal, expertise in program development, training opportunities, research, and advocacy must be mobilized and coordinated. Only then will each young person in out-of-home care have the opportunities and resources to develop the knowledge and skills necessary for productive adulthood.